A NATION'S HOPE

THE STORY OF BOXING LEGEND
JOE LOUIS

MATT DE LA PEÑA

illustrated by

KADIR NELSON

PUFFIN BOOKS
An imprint of Penguin Group (USA)

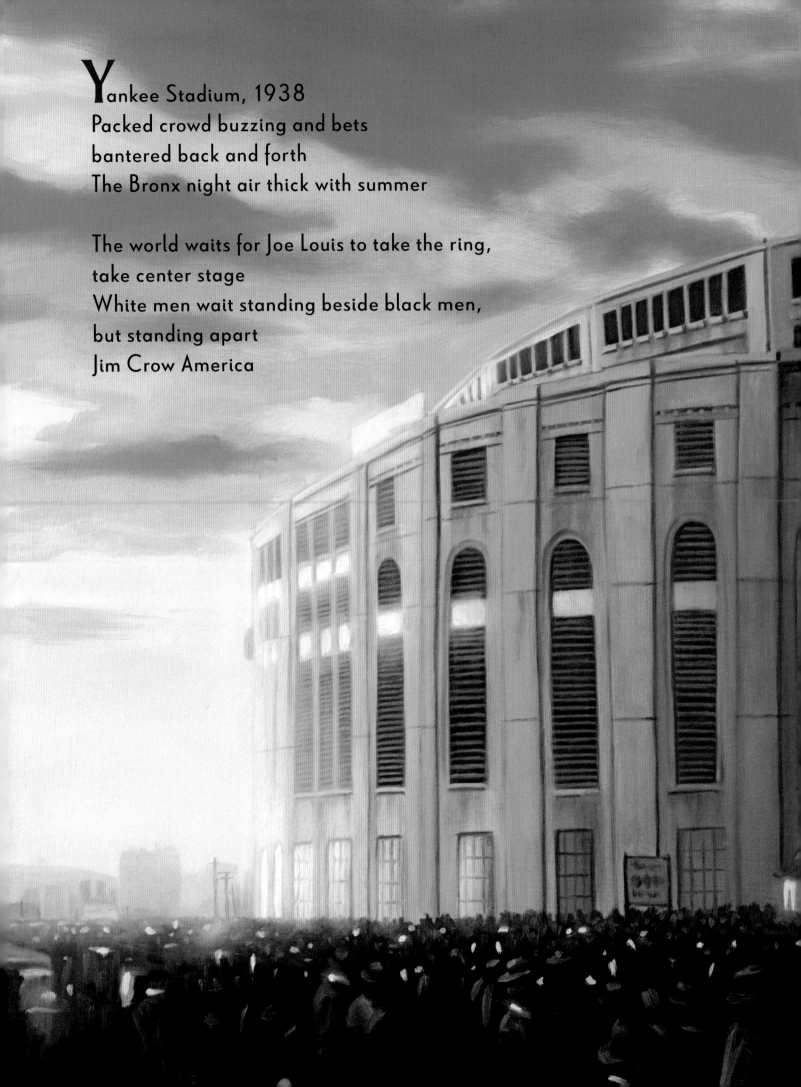

Yankee Stadium, 1938
Packed crowd buzzing and bets
bantered back and forth
The Bronx night air thick with summer

The world waits for Joe Louis to take the ring,
take center stage
White men wait standing beside black men,
but standing apart
Jim Crow America

JOE LOUIS

All to witness the most important
match in boxing history
Soft-spoken Joe Louis against the one man
who put him on his back

15 R

Joe LO

CHAMPIO

TADIUM

938 8:15 P. M.

MAX SCHMELING

os

UIS

MAX

But Joe knows tonight's fight is bigger
than any two men
Son of a black sharecropper
against Hitler's "master race"
Black and white Americans
together against the rule of Nazi hate

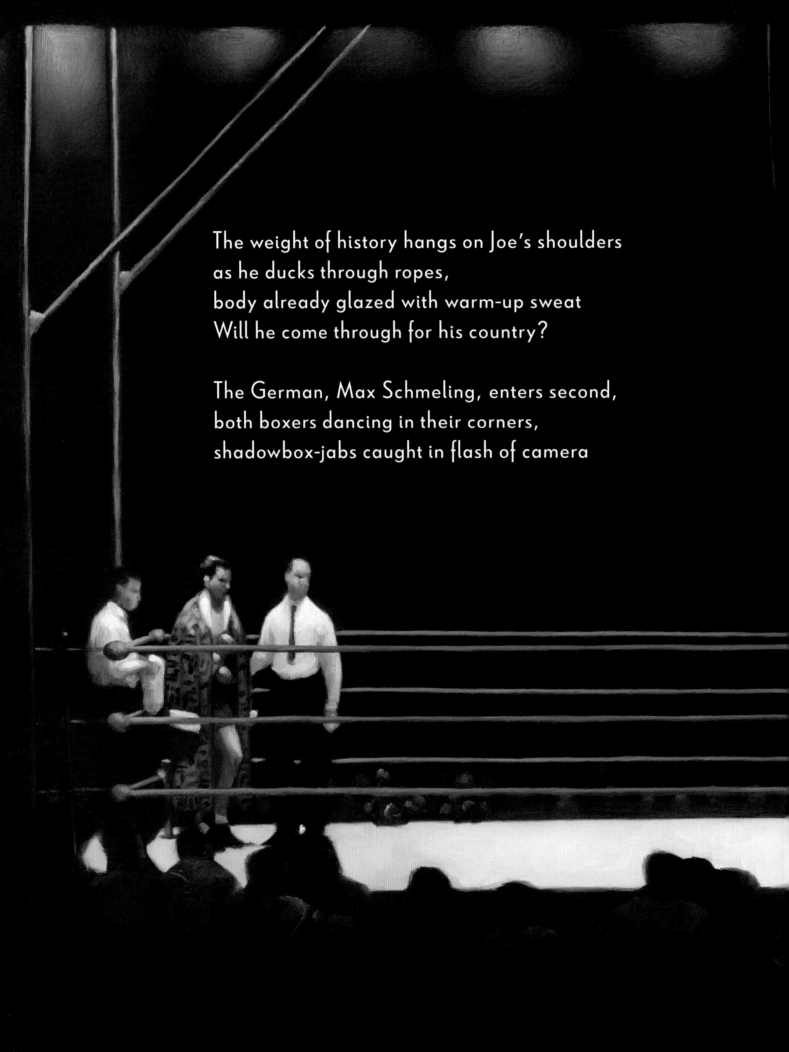

The weight of history hangs on Joe's shoulders
as he ducks through ropes,
body already glazed with warm-up sweat
Will he come through for his country?

The German, Max Schmeling, enters second,
both boxers dancing in their corners,
shadowbox-jabs caught in flash of camera

The referee calls the two to center ring
Biggest stage ever, he shouts over the crowd
May the best man win, he shouts

The bell dings and the two men raise fists,
come together under a deafening roar

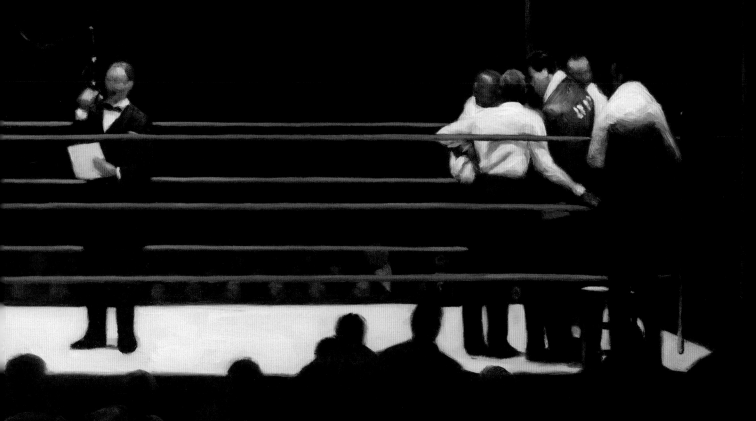

But the crowd didn't always roar
for Joe Louis

He didn't speak until he was six,
and when he finally spoke he stammered
and was ridiculed
Words spinning just beyond
Joe's grasp, and with black skin
he passed through childhood in shadows

Yet there was something about his hands,
so big and powerful
Nights he'd stare down at those hands and dream

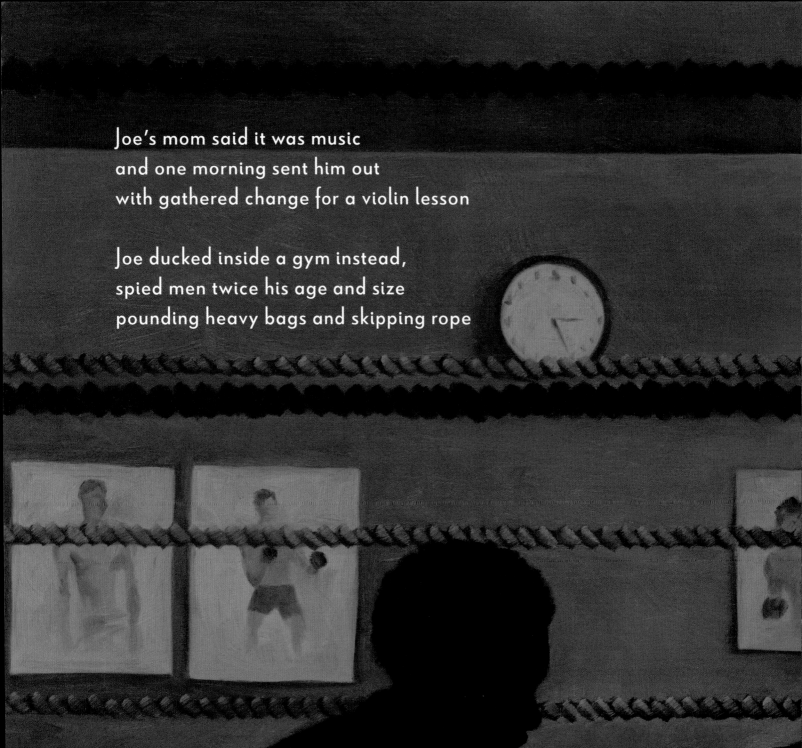

Joe's mom said it was music
and one morning sent him out
with gathered change for a violin lesson

Joe ducked inside a gym instead,
spied men twice his age and size
pounding heavy bags and skipping rope

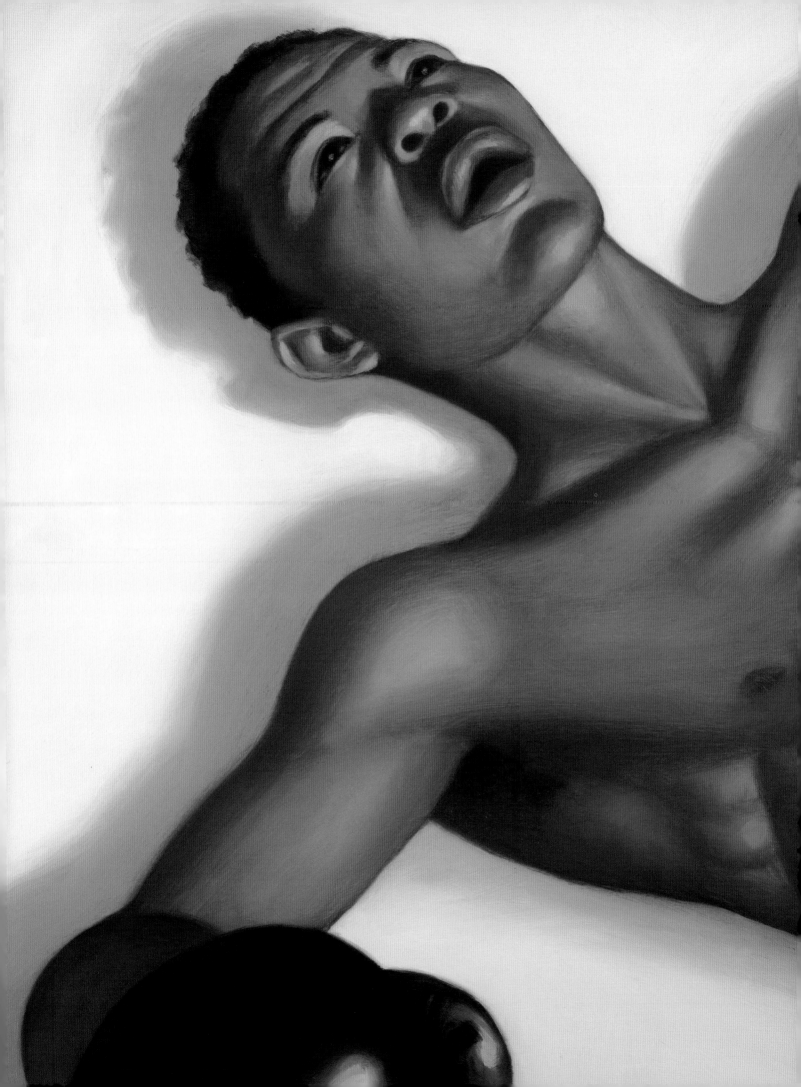

He returned, day after day,
slowly stepping out from shadows

First time inside a ring as an amateur, though,
his opponent was a blur of fists and footwork,
sent Joe toppling to the canvas seven times

Bruised jaw and bruised ego,
but Joe came back
He watched older boxers spar
and listened and grew into his body

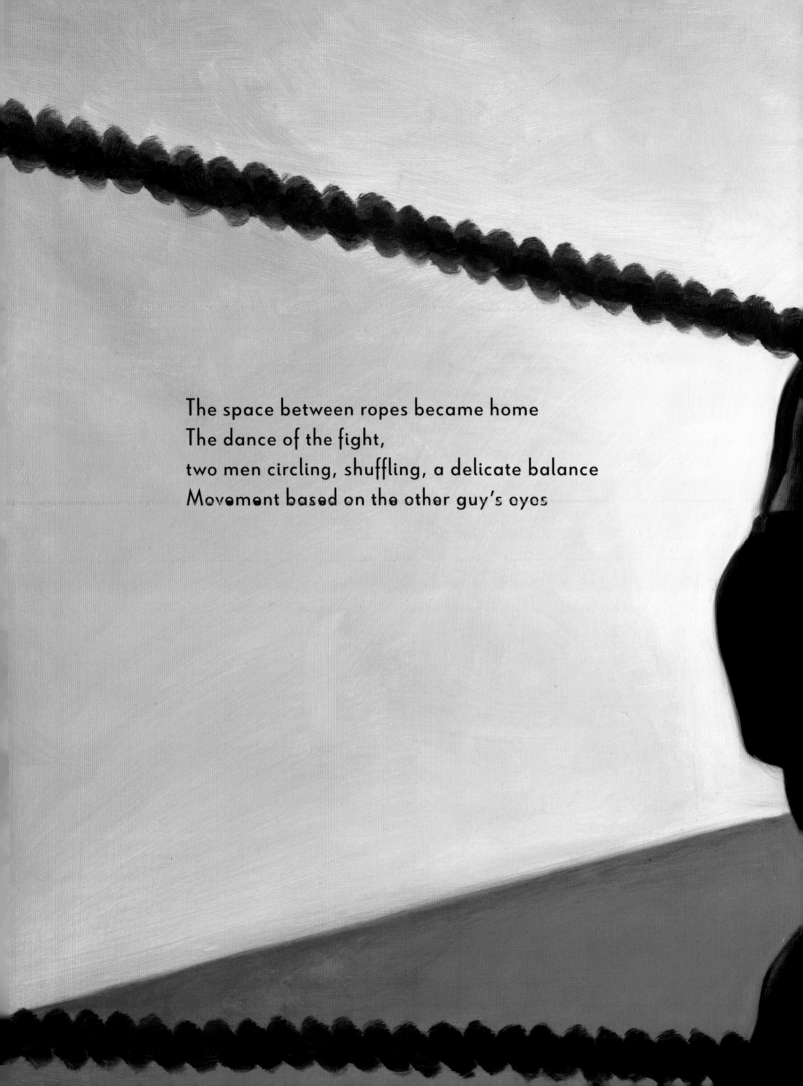

The space between ropes became home
The dance of the fight,
two men circling, shuffling, a delicate balance
Movement based on the other guy's eyes

Back then blacks didn't win decisions
Not against whites
Joe had to let his fists be the referees

In his first professional fight
he knocked a man clear out of the ring
But in victory Joe didn't raise his gloves and gloat,
he helped opponents to their feet
and shook their hands

More knockouts followed
Each new city, another fallen man
His legend quickly spread across the country,
people scrambling for a glance of Joe
in a cab or coming from a cafe

Louis to fight Baer

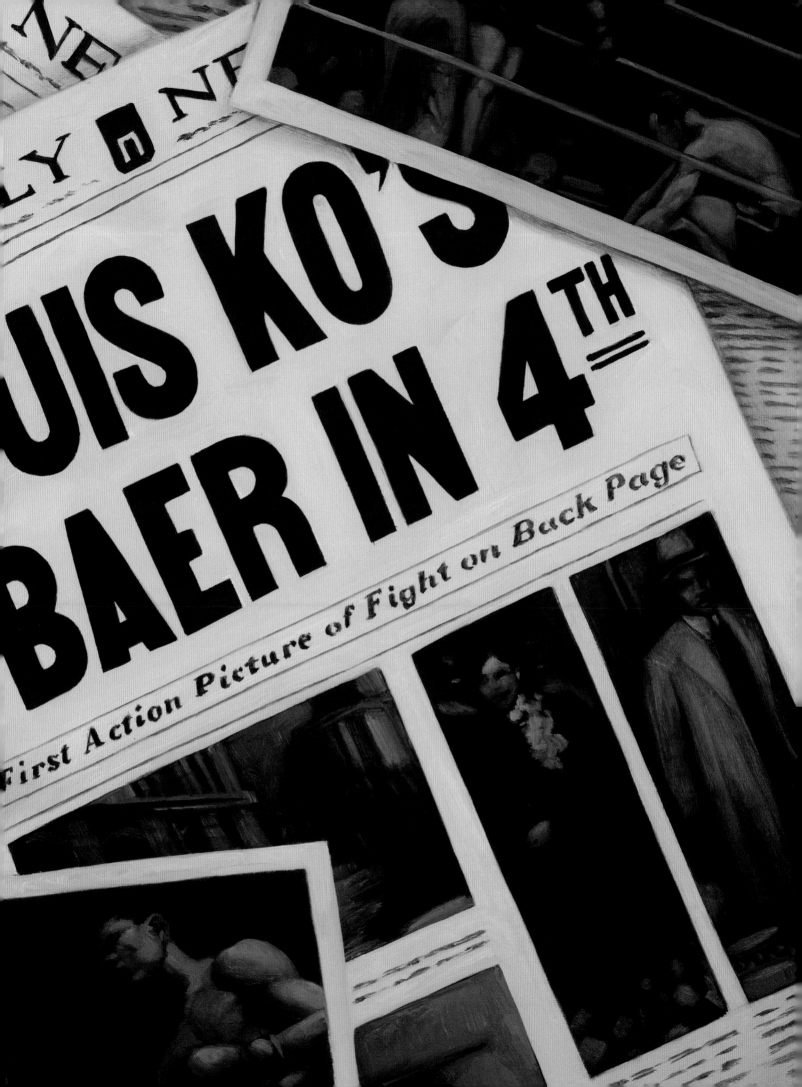

Black neighborhoods,
longing for a hero to call their own, found Joe,
and danced his every triumph in the streets
Hundreds surrounding Joe and his wife
down a Harlem sidewalk
Joe smiling, always humble
Waving back with those powerful hands,
once a boyhood dream, now a people's hope

But at the height of Joe's fame
Hitler's German caught him with his gloves down
and Joe woke up on his back

Devastated, he covered his face leaving the ring
Shadows once again falling and the taste of failure
Harlem streets struck silent

Joe healed and vowed to battle back
He worked even harder
as the world threatened war around him

Word leaked that the Nazis
were filling concentration camps in Europe
Just as Joe got another shot at the German

It was now more than just blacks who needed a hero,
it was all of America, and color was set aside

Seventy thousand erupt as Joe leaps
from his corner at the bell
An entire stadium leaning onto toes
and holding its breath

Ears glued to radio
in every home, in every city
The entire world stopping
Its fate seemingly all in Joe's hands

Instead of waiting this time,
Joe is first to strike
He jabs and retreats and jabs again,
his gloves never dropping an inch

He stings the German with an overhand right
and the crowd goes crazy
But Joe hears nothing
He strikes again, sends the German down

Soon as the German is up, Joe is on him again
A relentless fury of gloves and passion
The weight of the moment lifting,
shadows disappearing

The German goes down again and again,
until his corner man throws in the white towel
and the referee waves Joe away

Just like that it's over
Joe has shocked the world
The entire stadium in pandemonium,
white men hugging black men
and black men hugging back

The streets of Harlem once again dancing
for their hero

But all of America dancing this time

For Ryan, Baily, Maddy,
and Evey—M.d.

For Ali—K.N.

PUFFIN BOOKS
An imprint of Penguin Young Readers Group
Published by the Penguin Group
Penguin Group (USA)
375 Hudson Street
New York, New York 10014, U.S.A.

USA / Canada / UK / Ireland / Australia / New Zealand / India / South Africa / China
Penguin Books Ltd, Registered Offices: 80 Strand, London WC2R 0RL, England

For more information about the Penguin Group visit www.penguin.com

First published in the United States of America by Dial Books for Young Readers,
a division of Penguin Young Readers Group, 2011
Published by Puffin Books, an imprint of Penguin Young Readers Group, 2013

THE LIBRARY OF CONGRESS HAS CATALOGED THE DIAL BOOKS EDITION AS FOLLOWS:
Peña, Matt de la.
Joe Louis : a nation's hope / Matt de la Peña ; illustrated by Kadir Nelson. p. cm.
ISBN 978-0-8037-3167-7 (hardcover)
1. Louis, Joe, 1914–1981—Juvenile literature. 2. African American boxers—Biography—Juvenile literature.
I. Nelson, Kadir, ill. II. Title.
GV1132.L6P46 2011 796.83092—dc22 [B] 2010013477

Puffin Books ISBN 978-0-14-751061-7

Manufactured in China

11

The illustrations for this book were painted with oils on wood.

ALWAYS LEARNING

PEARSON